THE EUROPEAN UNION'S FUTURE

HEARING

BEFORE THE

SUBCOMMITTEE ON EUROPE, EURASIA, AND EMERGING THREATS

OF THE

COMMITTEE ON FOREIGN AFFAIRS HOUSE OF REPRESENTATIVES

ONE HUNDRED FOURTEENTH CONGRESS

FIRST SESSION

JULY 14, 2015

Serial No. 114–61

Printed for the use of the Committee on Foreign Affairs

Available via the World Wide Web: http://www.foreignaffairs.house.gov/ or http://www.gpo.gov/fdsys/

U.S. GOVERNMENT PUBLISHING OFFICE

95–514PDF   WASHINGTON : 2015

For sale by the Superintendent of Documents, U.S. Government Publishing Office
Internet: bookstore.gpo.gov Phone: toll free (866) 512–1800; DC area (202) 512–1800
Fax: (202) 512–2104   Mail: Stop IDCC, Washington, DC 20402–0001

CONTENTS

THE EUROPEAN UNION'S FUTURE

TUESDAY, JULY 14, 2015

HOUSE OF REPRESENTATIVES,
SUBCOMMITTEE ON EUROPE, EURASIA, AND EMERGING THREATS,
COMMITTEE ON FOREIGN AFFAIRS,
Washington, DC.

The subcommittee met, pursuant to notice, at 2:01 p.m., in room 2200, Rayburn House Office Building, Hon. Dana Rohrabacher (chairman of the subcommittee) presiding.

Mr. ROHRABACHER. I call to order the Europe, Eurasia, and Emerging Threats Subcommittee for this afternoon's hearing on the future of the European Union.

From a relatively modest idea in the early 1950s for six countries to form a common market for steel and coal production, the supranational organization that we now know as the European Union was created. Five and a half decades on, the European Union has expanded to include 28 national governments and represents over 500 million people. Taken together, the GDP of the EU is over $18 trillion, one of the largest global economies.

The historical forces which promoted the European integration after World War II helped to make that continent more peaceful and more prosperous. The European Union and the liberal values it embodies helped numerous post-Communist Eastern European countries make the transition from their Socialist Communist economies to a market economy. The fact that new countries continue to seek membership shows that the fundamental values of the EU are the right ones and continue to be attractive.

Despite this, however, the future of the European Union and the entire project of European integration has arguably never seemed so much in doubt. The EU has expanded to include economies of all sizes, countries, and different cultures, and sometimes conflicting national interests. This has led many to rightfully ask: Has the EU become too large to manage? Must more authority continue to be ceded to Brussels in order to prevent dysfunction?

While the negotiable agreement reached by the Greek Government yesterday appears to keep Greece in the eurozone for the time being, the crisis there is far from over. Greece's economy has shrunk by a quarter, and youth unemployment is 50 percent. And I hope the implementation of this latest agreement, which we saw yesterday, will set Greece on a better path. But, given the experiences of the past 5 years, I am certainly less than optimistic.

So let me just note, in 1953, Germany received a massive debt relief from its creditors. I can't help but wonder, if Greece received the same treatment 2 or 3 or 4 years ago, would we still be in this crisis moment that we see in Greece today? If questions about the integrity of the eurozone weren't enough, the authority and the legitimacy of the EU is also being challenged from within.

The popularity of basically Eurosceptic political parties has increased, and they are pushing back against the centralized power in Brussels. In last year's European Parliamentary election, over a quarter of the seats were claimed by Eurosceptics and Eurosceptic parties. In 2016, 2017, Great Britain, one of the largest EU countries, will hold an in-or-out referendum over the question of remaining in the European Union.

In the face of a major fiscal question and increasing doubts among the citizens of Europe, what then is the future of the EU? Have the influences, which historically drove integration, now are they driving people apart rather than bringing them together? Or is the answer to these difficulties to double down and to deepen the union to an even greater degree?

Before we go on, let me just note, I think the Greek crisis has an important lesson for our own country: A government can live beyond its means and live well on deficit spending, but not forever. And I hope lawmakers here in Washington, not just in the European capitals, have taken note of that fact.

So, with that said, I am looking forward to our witnesses. And I will turn now to the ranking member, Mr. Meeks, and then I will introduce the witnesses.

Mr. Meeks, you may proceed.

Mr. MEEKS. Thank you, Chairman Rohrabacher, and thank you for working with and putting this hearing together to provide us with an opportunity to openly examine current events in Europe and how they will shape the European Union's future.

The future, it seems, is becoming the present quickly. For many of us who work on Europe and related issues in this House, events within the EU have come into sharp focus. The issues being sorted out are not new, however. The United Kingdom has always had a special relationship with the continental Europe. The Greek economy did not begin to show troubling signs yesterday and the rise of extremist parties is not something new to Europe.

The question, therefore, is this: Are we seeing a restructuring of the European political system, or is this simply a necessary crack along the path to a more peaceful and united Europe? A prime example is the situation in Greece. This process is a reminder that the union is indeed a process and a club that demands cooperation, solidarity, and compromise. It is moments like what we have witnessed over this past weekend and into the early morning of yesterday that tests the mettle of the Union.

And I am encouraged by the fact that the parties came to an agreement for now and wish to see that the Greek Parliament make the necessary decisions in the upcoming days. Hopefully, in the future, such crises can be stemmed earlier in the game and not lead to brinkmanship involving such high stakes.

You know, I just returned from a trip to Riga, Latvia, where I discussed these issues with Latvian political leaders, their foreign ministers, citizens, and as well as with members of the European Parliament. They clearly see the benefits of a successful European

Union and an American presence on the continent. During the cold war, they lived on the other side under a regime that did not allow them the freedoms and prosperity they have today.

In Latvia, I also shared a meal with young American soldiers— some who happened to come from my State of New York—that represent our friendship and common values with Europe. On the ground, in people's lives, the future of Europe depends upon us working in partnership, America and our friends across the Atlantic. A united Europe represents American ideals along with European ideals and commerce and liberty and security that can lift standards all over the world.

Though difficult, times like these, I think that it is time that I believe that by working together we can ensure success. From the U.S. Congress' perspective, we understand the difficulties in creating a more perfect union, and we are still trying to move in that direction. But let us take a step back to define our important relationship with Europe and the European Union. The European project is a peace project firmly aligned with American interests and designed to promote liberal democratic ideals while working for the global common good.

Such a project may seem lofty, but in practice, it sets a framework to facilitate the free movement of people, commercial goods, finance, and ideas. This unprecedented and evolving union on the other side of the Atlantic consists of allies, our allies. And, of course, there is no roadmap for constructing the EU. Whether or not these mistakes could have been avoided is irrelevant at this time as we work together to iron out the remaining wrinkles in the European Union, working with them.

In our country, we are still perfecting our system of government and cooperation between the State and Federal levels, yet I believe that despite the difficulties of such an ambitious European Union, the will to do that is there. Despite the pain of reforms, the overwhelming majority of Greek citizens want to remain in the European Union. And we will find out what citizens of the United Kingdom think of their membership soon also. The internal affairs of the EU must be resolved so the integrity of the Union can continue to sustain its purposes.

So, with that, Mr. Chairman, I look forward to hearing the testimony of our witnesses as we talk more because we have all kinds of scenarios. When we talk about ISIS, China, we have got to work together with our allies across the Atlantic. I think that is tremendously important, and as so, there is plenty to do. And I would love to hear the testimony of our witnesses.

Mr. ROHRABACHER. Thank you very much, Mr. Meeks.

And, Mr. Sires, do you have a opening statement?

Mr. SIRES. I just want to say thank you for holding this hearing, and I want to hear what the witnesses have to say. Thank you.

Mr. ROHRABACHER. How about you, Colonel Cook?

Mr. COOK. I just have a brief statement since there was so much talk about Greece, and depending upon votes, some of my questions may orient toward that.

My big concerns right now are Russia. And Russia, which has been using oil and gas to control Europe, this is something that is not new. And, of course, if you look at the history and the cultural and historical ties, the Byzantine Empire, if you will, going back many, many years, long before I was born, I might add, that relationship kind of scares me, particularly the offer to help out the Greek economy. And that could drive a wedge between Greece, of course, and everything that is going on, and they might reorient themselves to Russia.

And so my questions, when we do get there, will be oriented toward that. As I said, I am very, very concerned about that, and not just the EU, but it is going to dwell into, of course, NATO.

So thank you very much for being here today. I am glad you had this hearing.

Mr. ROHRABACHER. Thank you very much, Colonel.

And we have three witnesses with us today. I would ask each of them to try to sort of put all of it down in about 5 minutes, if you could, and the rest you can submit for the record. But try to pick out the points that you really think are the most important for us to discuss. And then we will have, as I say, a dialogue afterwards.

Our friend from Alabama, Mr. Brooks, do you have an opening statement at all that you would like to make?

Mr. BROOKS. No, sir.

Mr. ROHRABACHER. All right. So, with that said, let me introduce our witnesses.

Dr. John McCormick is the Jean Monnet Professor of European Union Politics at Indianapolis campus of Indiana University. And he has authored over a dozen books, numerous journal articles. He was educated in Rhodes University in South Africa and University College London. All right.

And we have with us Steven Walt, the Robert and Renee Belfer Professor of International Affairs at Harvard's John F. Kennedy School of Government. And he is a contributing editor to Foreign Policy magazine and has authored four books on international affairs, including a New York Times bestseller.

And, finally, we have with us Dr. Jacob Kirkegaard, and he is a senior fellow at the Peterson Institute for International Economics. Previously, he worked with the Danish Ministry of Defense and the United Nations in Iraq. He studied at Columbia University, received a Ph.D. From Johns Hopkins University.

So we have three very prominent witnesses and people who are not only respected in the education but in foreign affairs as well, so we would be very appreciative of hearing what you have to say.

Dr. McCormick, you may begin.

STATEMENT OF JOHN MCCORMICK, PH.D., JEAN-MONNET PROFESSOR OF EUROPEAN UNION POLITICS, INDIANA UNIVERSITY-PURDUE UNIVERSITY INDIANAPOLIS

Mr. MCCORMICK. Well, good afternoon, and thank you very much for inviting me to this very topical hearing. My name is John McCormick. I am the professor of political science at the Indianapolis campus of Indiana University, and I have been studying, teaching, and writing about the European Union and its precursors for about 25 years.

In that time, the last decade, without question, has been the most challenging and the most troubled, beginning with the rejection of the constitutional treaty in 2005, moving to the global financial crisis that began in 2007, the eurozone crisis that began in 2009, which both evolved against a background of a growing popular reaction against European integration, a deep cynicism about the achievements of the European Union and doubts about its capacity to play a meaningful role in the world.

Regardless of all this, I remain the eternal optimist. I continue to believe very much in the many longer term achievements of the European Union: For example, the European single market and its many benefits; the role of integration in helping keep Europe at peace; the slow building of a Pan-European identity; the promotion of democracy and free markets, both at home and abroad; and everything from a cleaner environment to greater mobility for college students to cross-border police cooperation, common policies on trade and competition.

So we are here today to talk about the future of the European Union, but doing so is particularly difficult because of the nature of the raw material that we have to work with. And there are two particular problems that present themselves. First of all, we cannot agree on the political identity and personality of the European Union. It is very difficult to have a meaningful conversation and discussion about its successes and failures or about its future prospects when we don't know what "it" is.

Unfortunately, nobody has yet offered a definition of the European Union that can help us sort through these complexities. And when I am asked to answer the question, "What is the European Union?" My answer is, it is a confederal system with Federal qualities. And, unfortunately, that definition always demands subsidiary conversation about what exactly I mean, and it is not one with which many of my peers would anyway agree.

Second, much of the debate about the European Union and the effects of European integration is diverted by misunderstandings about the power and the reach of the European Union. Critics routinely overstate the powers of the European Union institutions. They routinely overstate the extent to which the laws of the member states are driven by the requirements of European Union law. They routinely blame the domestic problems of the member states on perfidious Brussels. And they often choose to focus more on the problems of the European Union, which make for dramatic headlines, than focusing on the successes, which don't.

So I was asked to comment specifically on three matters, and while I have done so in more detail in my written statement, I will just provide a very brief summary here. First of all, there is the question of the sovereign debt crisis in Greece. Many bright and creative minds have wrestled with the design and implementation of the euro and then with how best to respond to the debt crisis, and yet we still find ourselves in dire straits.

So predicting the future presents an enormous challenge. I do believe, though, that the crisis will be resolved; that all parties will adapt to the outcome; and we will learn and move on. Why? Very briefly, because the euro project is too big to fail, both politically and economically.

Secondly, there is the question of the U.K. Referendum on membership of the EU, and here I am on firmer ground. I predict firmly that the British people will vote to remain part of the European

Union. Why? Because the majority in favor of staying has been growing; because the referendum debate itself has been a learning experience that has drawn more attention to the benefits of staying and the costs of leaving; and because the Cameron Government has pledged to negotiate with forms of the European Union that may result in a further reduction in support for leaving. Now, we should also remember that the referendum is ultimately an effort to resolve a disagreement within the governing Conservative Party. And we should assess it as such.

Finally, there is the question of the electoral success of Eurosceptic political parties. It is true that they are attracting more support, but this is as much because of criticism of the political establishment in Europe and also as much about concerns about immigration as it is because of criticism of the European Union. And it is also important to appreciate that Euroscepticism comes in many different shades and that while some of its adherents wish to see their home states leave the European Union, many seek only reform of the European Union.

So, in conclusion, I would argue that the successes of the EU far outweigh its failures, that the governments of the member states will continue to work hard in the interest of European integration, and that the EU will weather the current storms and emerge bruised but wiser.

Thank you very much, again, for the opportunity to speak to you.

[The prepared statement of Mr. McCormick follows:]

Prepared statement of Dr. John McCormick
Jean Monnet Professor of European Union Politics
Department of Political Science
Indiana University-Purdue University Indianapolis

Given before the hearing on 'The European Union's Future'
Subcommittee on Europe, Eurasia, and Emerging Threats
Committee on Foreign Affairs
U.S. House of Representatives

July 14, 2015

Mr. Chairman and Members of the Subcommittee: thank you for convening this
hearing on the issue of the future of European Union, and for inviting me to provide
testimony. In your invitation, you noted that members of the subcommittee were
seeking to better understand the future of EU institutions and how they might
change in response to the Greek sovereign debt crisis, the referendum in the United
Kingdom, and the growing electoral success of euroskeptic political parties. It is my
pleasure to contribute the comments that follow.

Introduction

This hearing occurs at a deeply troubled and troubling time in the affairs of the
European Union. It has faced many crises since the process of European integration
formally began with the signature of the Treaty of Paris in April 1951, but none have
been so serious as the problems faced by the euro zone since the breaking of the
sovereign debt crisis in Greece in late 2009. Predictions regarding the outcome have
ranged from dire economic stress for Greece and other troubled euro states, to the
exit of Greece from the euro zone, to the collapse either the euro or of the European
Union itself.

The very range of these predictions is indicative of the uncertainties that attach to
any discussions about the present health and future prospects of the EU. While most
such discussions are currently shrouded in gloom, I remain optimistic for its future,
believe that a resolution will be found to the EU's current problems, and am
confident that it will emerge bruised but stronger from the present crisis. I would
also argue that it is particularly important in these troubled times not to lose sight of
the many and substantial achievements of European integration. I will address each
of the three topics listed by the subcommittee in turn.

The sovereign debt crisis in Greece

The debt crisis that broke in Greece in late 2009 has gone on to be the most harmful
and alarming of the many challenges faced by the process of European integration.
Earlier such challenges include the collapse in 1954 of plans to create a European

Defense Community, the unilateral French veto of the British application to join the European Economic Community (EEC) in 1963 and 1967, the 'empty-chair crisis' of 1965-66 when France withdrew from meetings of EEC bodies, the failure of early efforts to launch a single currency, the foreign policy embarrassments of the 1990s in the Gulf and the Balkans, and the collapse of the proposed constitutional treaty in 2005. Crisis has indeed been part of the evolution of European integration, but the EEC/EU has survived, learned, and moved on.

To some extent, the Greek debt crisis was predictable. Greece did not meet the criteria set for membership of the euro, including a limit on its budget deficit of 3 per cent of GDP. As a higher risk, it was obliged—before joining the euro—to borrow at higher interest rates than those charged to its wealthier EU neighbors, and much of its workforce had a long-standing reputation for tax avoidance; the OECD in 2009 estimated the size of the grey market in Greece to be equivalent to 25 per cent of the country's GDP. Once within the euro zone, it found that it could borrow at a cheaper rate than before, and banks were willing to lend. Greece's debt grew, its government misrepresented the size of that debt, many Greeks continued to avoid paying taxes, and the European Central Bank lacked the ability to review the budgets of euro member states.

Reforms were made in the wake of the crisis to EU policy and institutions. The European Central Bank now has stronger powers to monitor national budgets, a new institutional framework has been developed for financial supervision in the EU, and there have been efforts to build a European banking union. Mistakes have clearly been made in the response to the euro zone crisis, and there will be more adjustments in the wake of recent developments.

As for predicting the future, I could not claim to have the necessary expert understanding of monetary and fiscal policy enjoyed by economists, and I take heed of the lesson to be learned from two recent predictions by eminent voices. In 2012, Martin Feldstein—former chairman of the Council of Economic Advisors—argued that it was time to recognize the euro as an experiment that had failed.[1] A few months later, C. Fred Bergsten—chairman of the Competitiveness Policy Council—declared that fears of the collapse of the euro were 'vastly overblown', that adjustments had been made, and that once the dust had settled, the euro and the entire project of European integration was 'likely not only to survive but to emerge even stronger'.[2]

From the perspective of a political scientist, I believe that the crisis in the euro zone will be resolved, and that whether it involves a Greek exit from the euro zone or not, all parties will adapt to the outcome, and will learn and move on.

---

[1] Martin Feldstein (2012) 'The Failure of the Euro', in *Foreign Affairs* 91:1, Jan/Feb, pp. 105-16.

[2] C. Fred Bergsten (2012) 'Why the Euro will Survive', in *Foreign Affairs* 91:5, Sept/Oct, pp. 16-22.

The UK referendum

As we know, the Cameron government has promised to hold a referendum on continued UK membership of the EU, some time in 2016 or early 2017. The debate about the referendum is already well under way, and there has been much speculation about how it will evolve and about the likely result. Five points are particularly worth bearing in mind.

First, opinion polls dating back to 1977 have shown that the majority of British voters have consistently been in favor of their country remaining within the EEC/EU. There has been a notable reduction in the level of anti-EU sentiment since 2011, with the number wishing to leaving falling from 54 per cent in October 2011 to 25 per cent in June 2015, and the number wishing to remain within the EU growing over the same period from 46 per cent to 75 per cent. The failure of survey research accurately to predict the outcome of the May 2015 general election provides a cautionary tale, but the gap between those who support and those who oppose continued British membership of the EU is far outside any normal margin of error.

Second, the debate over the referendum has already sparked an informal public information program in which the pros and cons of EU membership are being aired and explored more intensively. Eurobarometer polls find that the British are notably badly informed about the EU and its powers: only half of those asked in a 2014 poll agreed with the statement 'I understand how the EU works'[3]. However, this was already a significant improvement on the same poll taken a year earlier, when the figure was 44 per cent.[4] As they become better informed, so British voters are likely to better understand many of the ways in which the powers and reach of the EU have been misrepresented by its critics. At the very least, it is possible that—as happened with the Scottish independence referendum in September 2014—many unanswered questions will be raised about the consequences of leaving the EU, and more voters will choose to err on the side of caution and cast ballots in favor of continued membership of the EU.

Third, part of the decline of opposition to membership can be explained by the evolution of the debate about the referendum so far, which has been characterized in particular by many statements from business and political leaders who have not previously made their views on the EU well known, and who have come out overwhelmingly in favor of the UK remaining within the EU. They have also often issued dire warnings of the potentially detrimental effects of a British exit.

Fourth, the Cameron government has long promised to renegotiate the terms of British membership of the EU prior to the holding of the referendum, and it is likely

---

[3] European Commission, Standard Eurobarometer poll 82, Autumn 2014.
[4] European Commission, Standard Eurobarometer poll 80, Autumn 2013.

that the revisions—and the prospect of wider reforms in the wake of the Greek debt crisis—will further strengthen support for continued membership.

Finally, it is important to appreciate that the referendum is driven in large part by an effort to end a harmful disagreement over Europe within the governing Conservative party. It is thus less an exercise in democracy than an exercise in political housekeeping, in much the same way as the last UK referendum on EEC membership, held in 1975, was concerned with ending a similar disagreement within the governing Labour party. Just over 67 per cent of voters opted to remain within the EEC in that referendum.

For all these reasons, and barring any dramatic international developments that might redirect the debate, I predict with a high degree of confidence that the referendum will result in a strong majority in favor of the UK remaining a member of the EU.

The electoral success of euroskeptic political parties

There is no question that euroskeptic political parties have been winning new support at elections in the member states of the EU. The successes of the National Front in France, of the UK Independence Party in Britain, and of the Party for Freedom in the Netherlands are well known. Much was also made of the gains by euroskeptic parties in the 2014 European Parliament elections.

However, the data must be treated with caution, for several reasons.

First, support for euroskeptic parties is more modest than the drama of news headlines would suggest, the numbers being clouded by the variety of policies supported by such parties, of which criticism of the EU is only one. The results of the 2014 European Parliament (EP) elections were widely hailed as a political earthquake, and yet voter turnout was only 43 per cent, and anti-establishment parties—defined broadly—won just 13 per cent of the vote. Furthermore, because EP elections are considered secondary to national elections, and are often used by voters to comment on national government, voters are more willing to use them to cast a protest vote, and preferences at EP elections do not carry over to national elections. The UK Independence Party, for example, won nearly 27 per cent of the vote in the 2014 EP elections in the UK, but only 13 per cent of the vote in the 2015 UK general election.

Second, euroskepticism is often portrayed as monolithic, as though all the supporters of eurosceptic parties were equally opposed to the EU and to the membership of their home states in the EU. But euroskepticism comes in many shades, and includes voters who oppose both the EU and the process of integration, as well as voters who support integration but believe in reform of the EU. In other words, euroskepticism does not preclude the possibility of supporting an EU that is more efficient, transparent, and accountable.

Third, euroskeptic parties are also populist parties, and populism throughout history has typically faded as quickly as it has blossomed. Populist parties either lose support or transform into mainstream parties with more mainstream policies. The initial excitement generated by support for a single issue or narrow range of issues quickly dissolves once a party is obliged to develop policy positions on a wider range of issues.

Finally, support for euroskeptic parties is not just a comment on the EU, but is also—for some voters, at least—a means for criticizing the political establishment. Party membership in Europe is on the decline, trust in government is on the decline, voters are using other means to participate in government, and the results of elections only tell part of the bigger story. Furthermore, support for euroskeptic parties overlaps with concerns about immigration, notably from Africa, the Middle East, and Asia. Immigration is arguably at least as important in the calculations of the supporters of euroskeptic parties as is hostility toward the EU.

Conclusions: The future of the EU and its institutions

Regrettably but understandably, the focus of the current debate about the European Union is on its difficulties and its crises. These are serious, to be sure, but we should not forget the many achievements of European integration, which have always been more enduring than its failures.

To quote the single example of the construction of the single market (a project favored even by most euroskeptics), it has been revolutionary in the changes it has wrought: time-consuming border crossings are mainly gone, new jobs have been created, business has access to a bigger marketplace, consumers have access to a wider range of products and services at more competitive prices, competition has encouraged innovation, technical standards and regulations have been improved and reduced, costly and protectionist national laws have been replaced with harmonized EU-wide approaches and standards, Europe's environment is cleaner, and the European market is today an irresistible economic magnet of a size and reach that allows the EU to exert soft influence on a global scale. The concern today is not that the single market has gone too far but that it has not gone far enough.

With achievements of this magnitude, the benefits of the EU will endure. Its institutions will continue to evolve as they have done since 1952. They work as well as can be expected given human nature and the unique personality of the European Union, their reach has expanded and changed as the effects of European integration have evolved, and there is no reason to suppose that they will not continue on this path indefinitely.

Mr. ROHRABACHER. Thank you, Dr. McCormick.

Dr. Walt.

STATEMENT OF STEPHEN WALT, PH.D., ROBERT AND RENEE BELFER PROFESSOR OF INTERNATIONAL AFFAIRS, BELFER CENTER FOR SCIENCE AND INTERNATIONAL AFFAIRS, JOHN F. KENNEDY SCHOOL OF GOVERNMENT, HARVARD UNIVERSITY

Mr. WALT. Mr. Chairman, Ranking Member Meeks, and members of the committee, it is an honor to speak with you today at this uncertain moment in European history. And given Europe's importance to the United States, trying to anticipate its future path is a critical task.

It is hard to be optimistic, however, about the EU's prospects. It has been a positive force in world politics for many years, but it suffers from growing tensions and self-inflicted wounds. It is likely to experience repeated crises and growing divisions, and we cannot rule out a gradual decline. Because a prosperous and tranquil Europe is in our interest, this is not good news for the United States.

As we have just heard, the European Union is in many ways a remarkable political achievement. Yet despite its past accomplishments, it faces five fundamental challenges, none easy to overcome. First, it is a victim of its past success. What began as a limited arrangement among six countries has become an elaborate supranational organization of 28 members. Those members are increasingly heterogeneous. Germany's GDP is 300 times larger than Malta's. Luxembourg's per-capita income is eight times higher than Latvia's, five times higher than Greece.

The size, population, and economic resources of these states varies enormously, as do their cultures and national histories. The expansion has made the EU more cumbersome and less popular. Two years ago, more than 70 percent of EU's citizens believed ''their voices do not count in EU decisionmaking.'' Nearly two-thirds believed ''the EU does not understand the needs of its citizens.''

Second, although the disappearance of the Soviet Union was a welcome development, it removed one of the main motivations for European unity. Since then, EU members have repeatedly pledged to develop a common, foreign, and security policy, but they have never done so. Today, the incoherent European response to events in Ukraine highlights the lack of consensus on basic security issues.

The third problem facing the EU today, of course, is the euro crisis. Seven years has passed since the crisis hit, and the EU still lacks the political institutions needed to sustain a genuine currency union. If Greece eventually exits, its departure will demonstrate the euro is not irreversible and so new doubts about its future. If Greece stays in, another crisis is probably inevitable.

Even worse, the crisis has sewn deep divisions within the continent, with debtors and creditors exhibiting a level of resentment and hostility not seen for many years. Needless to say, this is not what the euro's creators had in mind when they took that fateful step.

Fourth, the EU is now buffeted by serious regional turmoil. State failures in Africa and the Middle East have produced a flood of refugees seeking entry. Extremist movements, like Al Qaeda, have had worrisome repercussions among some of the Europe's Muslim population. The conflict in Ukraine raises new concerns about the eastern frontier. The EU has been unable to agree on new measures to address any of these challenges, further underscoring its dysfunctional decisionmaking.

The final challenge is the persistence of nationalism. The elites who built the EU hoped it would transcend existing loyalties. This has not occurred. Indeed, the United Kingdom may vote to leave the EU next year. Scotland may exit the United Kingdom. And national settlements continue to simmer in Catalonia and elsewhere.

Now, economic hardship and rising concerns about immigration are reinforcing the emergence of Eurosceptic parties that reject the basic ideas on which the EU was built. And you add to that mix Europe's unfavorable demography—its population is declining, and the median age is rising rapidly—and you have a recipe for continued economic stagnation, which will, of course, encourage the prospects of some of these nationalist parties.

Looking ahead, you can imagine at least three possible futures for the EU. First, in theory, bold leadership could build the institutions needed to support the euro, assimilate new immigrants, adopt reforms to produce stronger economic growth. But that is unlikely. No European leaders today have the vision and stature of an Adenauer, de Gaulle, or Thatcher. Serious reforms would take years to implement given the EU's elaborate machinery.

Instead of an ever greater Union, therefore, the EU is more likely to simply muddle through. It will try to contain the fallout from the euro crisis, hope new trade deals with the United States and with China will provide an economic boost. In this scenario, the EU survives, but its global influence declines.

But there is a third possibility: The entire experiment could begin to unravel. A Greek exit would set a dangerous precedent. Nationalist sentiments could deepen. New authoritarian leaders could come to power. Greece or Hungary might even draw closer to Moscow. And once that process begins, the only question would be, how far and how fast will it go?

Lastly, both muddling through or a gradual unravelling would be bad news for the United States. Slow growth in Europe means slow growth here in the United States. A weaker Europe will be less useful as the United States tries to deal with a rising China or a turbulent Middle East.

To sum it up: Since the end of World War II, stability and prosperity in Europe have been a great benefit to the United States. And the EU has been a key ingredient in a world order that was very favorable for the United States.

But if the EU's best days are behind it, Americans will have to prepare for a world that is less stable, less secure, less prosperous than the one to which we have become accustomed. I hope that is not the case, but that is the most likely outcome, given where we are today.

Thank you very much.

[The prepared statement of Mr. Walt follows:]

The Future of the European Union
Stephen M. Walt
Robert and Renee Belfer Professor of International Affairs
John F. Kennedy School of Government
Harvard University

Testimony to the Committee on Foreign Affairs
Subcommittee on Europe, Eurasia and Emerging Threats
U.S. House of Representatives
Hearing on "The European Union's Future"
July 14, 2015

Mr. Chairman, Ranking Member Engel, and members of the Committee:
It is an honor to be invited to speak with you today, in the company of these other experts. It is obviously a tumultuous time for the nations of Europe, most of whom are close allies of the United States. Because the European Union is a key trading partner, home to more than 500 million people, and tied to the United States through NATO and many other connections, its condition is of obvious importance to the United States. Trying to anticipate its future path is therefore a critical task.

Unfortunately, it is hard to be optimistic about the EU's long-term prospects. Although the EU has been a positive force in world politics for many years, it now suffers from growing structural tensions and a series of self-inflicted wounds. Its members may overcome today's challenges and continue to build an "ever-closer union," but this outcome is unlikely. Instead, the EU is more likely to face repeated crises and growing internal divisions, and we cannot rule out the possibility of gradual and irreversible disintegration. This situation is not good news for the United States, as it will make Europe a less valuable ally and increase the number of places and issues that U.S. leaders need to worry about.

To explain why I reach this depressing conclusion, I first describe the EU's past achievements and then discuss the main sources of strain it now faces. I close by outlining several possible futures and explain why I believe the EU's best days are behind it.

Past Achievements

The European is in many ways a remarkable political experiment. In the aftermath of the most destructive war in history, and after centuries of recurring conflict, a generation of European leaders had the imagination and determination to conceive and create a new order based on economic integration, open borders, and the partial surrender of sovereignty to a new supranational organization. The original European Coal and Steel Community evolved to become the European Common Market, expanded to include a host of new entrants, and then deepened to become the European Union and create a common currency for some of its members.

For much of the past half-century, this collective effort encouraged economic growth, gave Europe a more coherent voice in international economic affairs, and reduced the danger of great power competition in Europe itself. The EU has also been an influential model for other states, and especially the post-communist governments in Eastern Europe. Indeed, the desire for EU membership encouraged these states to adopt critical democratic reforms following the collapse of the Soviet Union and dampened potential conflicts during this delicate transition period.

Yet despite these impressive accomplishments, the EU's present condition and future prospects are not bright. In particular, it now faces at least five fundamental challenges. Some of these challenges are problems of its own creation; others reflect broader changes in the world at large. None of them will be easy to overcome.

Sources of Strain

1. Over-Expansion

The EU is now a victim of its past successes. What began as a limited arrangement among six countries to coordinate the production and marketing of coal and steel has become an elaborate supranational organization with twenty-eight members, whose affairs are partially governed by the European Commission, the Council of Europe, the European Parliament, the European Council and its elected president, the European Court of Justice, and a host of subsidiary agencies. Each member-state retains a separate national government, however, with authority over health, police, fiscal policy, and defense and foreign policy. Today, Europe's governance arrangements make America's federal system look simple by comparison.

Moreover, as the EU has grown, its membership has become increasingly heterogeneous in terms of population, economic size, per capita income, and cultural background. At roughly €2 trillion, Germany's GDP is more than three hundred times larger than Malta's (€6 billion), while Luxemburg's per capita income is roughly eight times larger than Latvia's and five times larger than that of Greece. The geographic size, population, and natural resource endowments of the EU's member states also vary enormously, as do their cultures, religious affiliations, and national histories.

Ironically, that heterogeneity is a key reason why the EU's newest members (mostly from East and Southeastern Europe) were eager to join, and why the original members encouraged their aspirations. In essence, both parties wanted the new member states to become more like the rest of the community. But convergence between old and new members has been slow and incomplete, and the EU's governing institutions must try to accommodate and reconcile a broader array of interests, political traditions and historical experiences than it did in earlier periods. The inevitable result is that harder for the EU to reach consensus on critical issues and more difficult to resolve underlying problems in a timely and effective manner.

As the EU has grown, in short, it has become more cumbersome, more divided, and less effective. It has also become less popular, with more than 70 percent of EU citizens reporting in

2013 that "their voices do not count in EU decision-making" and nearly two-thirds declaring "the EU does not understand the needs of its citizens."[1]

2. The Demise of the Warsaw Pact

The disappearance of the Soviet Union was a welcome development, but it removed one of the main motivations for European unity. Although scholars and journalists often portray the EU as a purely economic and political project, security concerns were a key part of its rationale from the start.[2] In particular, European leaders in the 1950s believed only a continental-scale economy could provide the wherewithal to counter the Soviet Union and Warsaw Pact, and economic integration was also necessary to prevent political rivalries from undermining the Western effort to keep communism from spreading. Together with NATO, therefore, European economic integration was an important component of the Western effort to contain Soviet expansion.

This security rationale faded as NATO become stronger and it disappeared entirely when the Soviet Union collapsed. The absence of a clear and present danger permitted Europe's leaders to focus more attention on individual national concerns, and devote less political capital to preserving the broader European project. EU members have repeatedly pledged to develop a "common foreign and security policy," but they have never succeeded in doing so. Today, the incoherent and inconsistent European response to events in Ukraine highlights the lack of consensus among EU governments on basic foreign policy issues.

3. The Euro Crisis

The third problem facing the EU today is the euro crisis. With hindsight, it is clear the decision to create the euro was a fateful error, as skeptics from across the political spectrum warned at the time. European leaders established a common currency for political rather than economic reasons: they sought to give new momentum to the broader goal of European unity, to bind a reunified Germany within a stronger set of European institutions, and to put Europe on a more equal footing with the United States.

But as the euro's critics emphasized, the EU did not possess the political and institutional mechanisms needed to make a currency union work. Instead, the euro's proponents simply assumed that eurozone members would abide by agreed-upon fiscal guidelines and never allow themselves to get into serious financial trouble. As Joseph Joffe, the editor of Die Zeit, noted back in 1997, the euro tied the disparate national economies together like cars on a locomotive and assumed that all would run at the same speed and on the same track forever.[3] The euro's architects further assumed that if these assumptions proved to be too optimistic (as indeed they did), a future crisis would force them to create the political and economic institutions they

---

[1] Pew Research Center, "Key Takeaways from the European Union Survey," May 12, 2014, at http://www.pewresearch.org/fact-tank/2014/05/12/5-key-takeaways-from-the-european-union-survey/

[2] See Sebastian Rosato, Europe United: Power Politics and the Making of the European Community (Ithaca: Cornell University Press, 2012).

[3] Joseph Joffe, "The Euro: The Engine That Couldn't," New York Review of Books, December 4, 1997, at http://www.nybooks.com/articles/archives/1997/dec/04/the-euro-the-engine-that-couldnt/

needed (e.g., common bank regulations, shared fiscal policy, a stronger central bank, and greater capacity to transfer resources from wealthy states to members in need of help).
The 2008 financial crisis exposed their follies and the EU has been preoccupied with containing the damage ever since. Seven years have passed since the crisis hit and top government officials and central bankers are still devoting countless hours to saving the common currency. They have made tentative steps toward creating slightly stronger economic institutions, but the EU is still light-years away from having the political institutions needed to sustain a genuine currency union. When Greece exits—as it almost certainly will—this event will demonstrate that the euro is not irreversible and sow new doubts about its long-term prospects.

The economic costs of the euro crisis have been enormous, but the political costs are also substantial. Every hour that Europe's leaders have spent trying to dig themselves out of this mess is an hour they could not devote to dealing with China's rise, the problem of terrorism, the consequences of the so-called Arab spring, Russia's policy in Ukraine, or any number of domestic issues. Even worse, the euro crisis has sown deep divisions within the continent itself, as debtors and creditors increasingly regard each other with a level of resentment and hostility not seen for many years. Needless to say, this situation is not what the euro's creators had in mind when they took that fateful step.

4. A Deteriorating Regional Environment

The EU is now buffeted by serious instability on its frontiers. State failures in Libya, Syria, Yemen, and parts of Africa have produced a growing flood of refugees seeking to enter the EU, while the emergence of Al Qaeda, ISIS and other extremist movements has had worrisome repercussions among small percentage of Europe's Muslim population. While it is sometimes exaggerated, the danger of home-grown terrorism is not zero and a number of Europeans are now calling for new barriers to immigration and new limits on cross-border movements within Europe itself. If adopted, such measures would reverse the movement toward open borders that was one of the singular achievements of the 1986 Single European Act. Last but not least, continued violence in Ukraine raises new concerns about the security of the EU's eastern frontier. EU member-states have thus far been unable to agree on new measures to address any of these challenges, further underscoring the dysfunctional nature of contemporary EU decision-making.

5. The Persistence of Nationalism

The elites who created and built the EU hoped that it would transcend existing national loyalties and that its citizens would eventually identify as Europeans first and as Germans, Danes, Italians, Belgians, Spaniards, etc. second. This transformation of loyalties has not occurred; if anything, public attitudes are headed the other way. As previously discussed, the euro crisis has exacerbated national tensions and European leaders have consistently emphasized national interests rather than the broader goal of European unity, even as they attempt to strengthen the EU's existing institutions.[4] The United Kingdom may even vote to leave the EU next year, while

---

[4] This behavior is not new; earlier steps to build stronger institutions invariably involved bargains between competing state interests. See Andrew Moravcsik, The Choice for Europe: Social Purpose and State Power from Messina to Maastricht (Ithaca: Cornell University Press, 1998).

resurgent nationalism could lead Scotland to exit the United Kingdom. Powerful nationalist sentiments continue to simmer in Catalonia and several other regions as well.

Economic hardship and rising opposition to immigration have also fueled a resurgence of extreme right-wing movements in many European states. These movements are hostile to the core principles upon which the EU is built and their growing popularity raises further doubts about the EU's long-term future. Add to this mix Europe's unfavorable demography—its population is declining and the median age is rising rapidly—and you have a recipe for continued economic stagnation and popular discontent. If these trends bring parties such as France's National Front to power, it will make it even harder for the EU to regain its former legitimacy and restore momentum for further integration.

What Lies Ahead?

Looking forward, one can imagine at least three possible futures for the European Union. First, Europe's current leaders could follow in their predecessors' footsteps and find new ways to overcome the challenges identified above. Support for European integration has waxed and waned in the past, but previous European politicians eventually opted to move forward rather than let their grand experiment languish or collapse. In theory, creative and determined leadership could save the euro (with or without Greece), build the institutions needed to support a common currency, integrate immigrant populations more effectively, and adopt reforms designed to trigger more vigorous economic growth across the continent. Concerns about Russia's intentions might provide a new rationale for unity as well, and especially if the trouble in Ukraine spreads to other areas.

Unfortunately, this optimistic vision of a reinvigorated EU is unlikely to occur. There are no European leaders today with the vision and stature of a Konrad Adenauer, Charles DeGaulle, or Margaret Thatcher, and European publics are more likely to reward politicians who secure better deals for their individual countries rather than those who sacrifice narrow interests in favor of an ever-closer union. The EU's elaborate governance structures would make any serious reform effort a long and torturous process, which means even a successful resurgence is likely to take years to design and implement.

Instead of a new push for ever-greater union, therefore, the EU is more likely to simply muddle through. It will strive to contain the fallout from a Grexit, sign the Transatlantic Trade and Investment Partnership (TTIP) with the United States and pursue closer economic ties with China.

If all goes well, the EU will still be in business, but its current liabilities will remain and its global influence will continue to decline.

There is a third possibility, however: the EU experiment could begin to unravel in more far-reaching ways. Greece's exit from the Eurozone will create new doubts about the euro's future, more member-states may begin to question the benefits of membership and a few (such as Greece or Hungary) might even draw closer to Moscow. Nationalist resentments could fester and deepen, authoritarian or neo-fascist leaders could come to power somewhere, and Greece or

Hungary might even draw closer to Moscow. If the EU begins to unravel, the only question may be: how fast and how far?

Neither "muddling through" nor gradual collapse would be good news for the United States. Europe is not as vital a strategic interest as it was during the height of the Cold War, but it is still an important economic and military partner. Slow growth in Europe also means slower growth here in the United States, and a divided and poorer Europe will be even less helpful as the United States tries to deal with a rising China, a turbulent Middle East, or instability in sub-Saharan Africa. Problems within the EU will distract us, and reduce the time and attention US leaders can devote to other issues.

To sum up: since the end of the Second World War, tranquility and prosperity in Europe has been of enormous benefit to the United States. The European Union was not the only source of stability and economic growth in Europe, but it was a key ingredient in a world order that was overwhelmingly favorable for the United States. If the EU's best days are behind it—and there are good reasons to believe that they are—then Americans must prepare for a world that is less stable, secure and prosperous than the one to which we have become accustomed. I hope that is not the case, but it is the most likely outcome given where we are today.

Thank you.

Mr. ROHRABACHER. Well, we have heard from the optimist and the pessimist.

And now do you have a fusion position for us, Doctor?

STATEMENT OF JACOB FUNK KIRKEGAARD, PH.D., SENIOR FELLOW, PETERSON INSTITUTE FOR INTERNATIONAL ECONOMICS

Mr. KIRKEGAARD. Mr. Chairman, Ranking Member Meeks, members of the committee, it is a pleasure to testify before you today.

In my oral testimony, I will address three impacts on the European Union's future: First, from the Greek sovereign debt crisis; then from the upcoming United Kingdom referendum on EU membership; and, finally, on the growing electoral success on Eurosceptic parties.

The Greek sovereign debt crisis is first and foremost a crisis for the euro area. Relative to existing Pan-EU institution, recent developments have essentially cemented the existence of a multispeed Europe where countries in the euro area have undertaken dramatic new integration while other member states remaining outside the common currency are only affected to a limited degree.

Recalling, however, that this multispeed situation has been de facto present in the EU for many decades, there is no obvious reason to fear that the existing new institutions cannot continue to cope with this situation also going forward.

Recent events over the weekend saw a dramatic escalation in the confrontation between the Greek Government and the rest of the euro area. Negotiations took place with a major taboo in the euro area of politics, the possible exit of a member state from the common currency broken, and Alexis Tsipras for the first time faced this political calamity for Greece. He subsequently, in my opinion, quite understandably, folded his position.

The decision, however, by the euro area to make the possibility of exit from the common currency an explicit and obviously very effective negotiating tool will have changed the nature of the euro currency itself. Given the willingness of top euro area political leaders to use this exit threat, the irreversibility of the common currency in all member states is today less certain and subject to a higher degree of political uncertainty.

This will significantly have increased the political and financial onus on the euro area to agree to more and deeper institutional integration of the euro area in the short to medium term. Recent events in Greece therefore can be expected to lead to a further accelerated integration of the euro area, though, as mentioned, not have direct implications for the EU as a whole.

The upcoming U.K. Referendum on EU membership is highly unlikely, in my opinion, to lead to material and lasting changes to EU institutions for the simple reason that the referendum is overwhelmingly likely to be fought with the U.K. Government, the Prime Minister, and all the main bridge opposition parties all campaigning successfully for the U.K. To remain in the EU.

David Cameron and the U.K. Government will campaign, in my opinion, for a yes to avoid severing the ties between the Conservative Party and its traditional funding base in the British business, as well as to avoid the results in economic uncertainty and damage to the U.K. Economy from a no vote. Similarly, the referendum will take place in a favorably economic context of a projected growth between 2 and 2.5 percent between now and 2016, which is the most likely year for the referendum.

Most importantly, however, the politically necessary changes to EU law will be possible for David Cameron to achieve. In principle, EU law is valid throughout the 28 member states, yet in a number of cases, individual member states have secured so-called legal opt-out for specific elements of the EU treaty, exempting them from having to implement some policies at home.

In short, the EU legal framework is a highly flexible animal when EU leaders require such flexibility and legal finessing to overcome a particular political problem. Given how Germany and many other EU members have already expressed their clear political interests in seeing the U.K. Remain a member of the EU, there can, in my mind, be no doubt that the full arsenal of legal EU flexibility around the EU treaty will be made available to David Cameron.

There will, consequently, in my opinion, be ample opportunities for the Prime Minister to secure politically important as well as legally binding changes to the EU laws governing the economy at the United Kingdom as part of the now ongoing negotiation, all of which points to a yes vote in the referendum and therefore largely maintaining the institutional status quo within the EU.

In recent years, many EU countries have witnessed the growth of new parties that can be classified as broadly anti-establishment and Eurosceptic in their political outlook. At the same time, however, it is important to recognize that European parliamentary systems have historically often operated very successfully with very large anti-establishment representation at national and European levels.

Prior to 1989, this was often seen with an often sizable Communist Party representation in national legislatures. There is, therefore, a priori no reason to believe that current levels of representation of these types of parties in EU Parliament represent a historically unprecedented and impossible situation.

There is further no immediate reason to believe to Eurosceptic parties are going to continue to grow beyond their historical political range of up to about 25 percent of public support and into effective governing majorities across Europe. This is due to the narrowness of the core shared both left- and right-wing populist message of many of these parties, which can best be described as a welfare chauvinistic political platform that at once advocates a strong and activist role for the government in protecting the social welfare but only so for the native population.

This policy mix has generally and successfully targeted the lower skill segments of European electorates yet has to date failed to extend much beyond these groups and into a genuine majoritarian platform. Yet, even without the prospects of gaining governing power, the stronger political voices of these parties very significantly raise the political hurdles for further revisions of the EU treaty.

This means that the EU for the foreseeable future will have to continue to function within the broad legal framework laid down in the 2009 Lisbon Treaty. In sum, therefore, the recent reemergence of these Eurosceptic and anti-establishment parties across Europe will not materially affect the overall direction of EU policies but will greatly slow down the adaptability of the EU's existing institutional design to future challenges.

In summary, therefore, the overall state of the EU is challenged but nonetheless remain more stable than is often believed. Thank you very much.

[The prepared statement of Mr. Kirkegaard follows:]

Congressional Testimony

The European Union's Future

Jacob Funk Kirkegaard, Senior Fellow, Peterson Institute for International Economics

Testimony before the U.S. House of Representatives Subcommittee on Europe, Eurasia and Emerging Threats, July 14, 2015

Subcommittee Chairman Royce, ranking member Engel, members of the Subcommittee on Europe, Eurasia and Emerging Threats, it is a pleasure to testify before you today on the future of the European Union. In my written testimony, I will in line with the hearing invitation address three issues: The impact on European Union institutions from the Greek sovereign debt crisis; the impact on European institutions from the upcoming United Kingdom referendum on EU membership; and the impact on EU institutions of the growing electoral success of euro-skeptic parties.

The Impact on European Institutions of the Greek Sovereign Debt Crisis

The Greek sovereign debt crisis is first and foremost a crisis for the euro area, as it has since 2010 highlighted fundamental flaws in the original institutional design of the common currency laid down in the early 1993 Treaty of Maastricht. Appropriately since 2010, the euro area has as part of the European crisis response undergone a dramatic institutional deepening. A new fiscal rescue fund (e.g. a de facto Euro Area Monetary Fund) in the ESM has been created with enough financial firepower (€500bn) and freedom of action to directly rescue banks and lend sufficiently and conditionally to governments to stabilize their finances in any new emergency. The ECB has introduced a new "conditional lender of last resort" function through its OMT program, which guarantees any member state access to potential future emergency support (e.g. sovereign bond purchases) of the ECB in return for undertaking a conditional program of economic reforms. The euro area has introduced a new single banking supervisor and a single resolution mechanism will become operational by 2016. In short, the Greek sovereign debt crisis, as well as the crises in other euro area members since 2010, has led to a historic further institutional deepening of the common currency area.

Relative to the existing EU institutions, recent developments have cemented the existence of a multi-speed Europe, where the countries in the euro undertake dramatically more integration, while other member states remain on outside the common currency and only affected to a limited degree. The majority of recent crisis related euro area institutional deepening has taken place legally outside the existing EU Treaty framework through a number of inter-governmental Treaties, such as the ESM Treaty[1]

---

[1] http://www.esm.europa.eu/pdf/ESM%20Treaty%20consolidated%2003-02-2015.pdf

or the Treaty on Stability, Coordination and Governance in the Economic and Monetary Union[2]. Recalling, however, that this multi-speed situation has been de facto present in the EU for decades and with respect to EMU since the inception of the euro in the early 1990s, there is no obvious reason to fear that existing EU institutions cannot cope with this situation also going forward. This view is underlined by the creation of the new banking union, which while a matter of life and death for the euro area, is also an urgently important reform for the rest of the EU. The banking union, which in the euro area has seen the transfer of banking supervisory functions to the ECB, also includes establishing much closer banking regulatory integration for the entire EU in the rules making European Banking Authority (EBA). As part of this setup, obvious fears existed among the non-euro members that their regulatory and rules making concerns would be trumped by the now dominant euro area single supervisor at the ECB. However, as a result the EU banking regulatory process has now been established with extensive "minority protections" built into the system to protect the voice of the non-euro area members. Regulatory decisions normally taken by a simple or qualified majority vote (on a one member one vote basis) now requires support by a simple majority of both participating and non-participating member states in the banking union to be adopted[3]. Dramatic institutional integration of the euro area banking sector has thus been achieved in the banking union without jeopardizing the national sovereignty of non-euro area members in the process.

Recent events over the weekend saw a dramatic escalation in the confrontation between the Greek government and the rest of the euro area. Ultimately, the tentative agreement struck very late Sunday saw a climb down by the Greek government on almost all policy areas[4]. This was a result of the disastrous Greek government decision to call a referendum on its bailout conditions on July 5th. The referendum produced a result – a resounding no! – interpreted elsewhere in the euro area as the desire by the Greek public to distance themselves from the euro. This political interpretation for the first time opened for the broader political acceptance in many euro area countries that Greek might have to leave the common currency. As a result, this weekend's negotiations took place with a major taboo in euro area politics – the possible exit from euro area institutions of a member state – broken, and Alexis Tsipras for the first time faced this potential economic and political calamity for Greece. His subsequent agreement to the terms of the euro area is both understandable and commendable.

Yet, the decision by the euro area to make the possibility of exit from the common currency area an explicit – and obviously extremely effective – negotiating tool will have changed the nature of the euro currency itself. Given the willingness of the top euro area political leaders to use his threat, the irreversibility of the common currency in all member states is less certain today, and subject to a higher degree of political uncertainty. This will potentially complicate the conduct of monetary policy in the euro area going forward, and especially potentially raise the risks associated with ending the current asset purchase program of the ECB as scheduled in September 2016. It cannot be ruled out that financial

---

[2] http://europa.eu/rapid/press-release_DOC-12-2_en.pdf
[3] For details, see http://europa.eu/rapid/press-release_MEMO-13-780_en.htm?locale=en
[4] http://www.consilium.europa.eu/en/press/press-releases/2015/07/pdf/20150712-eurosummit-statement-greece/?utm_source=DSMS&utm_medium=email&utm_campaign=Euro+Summit+Statement+12%2f07%2f2015&utm_term=952.30436.1082.0.30436&utm_content=all+customers

markets may then once again add a certain degree of re-domination risk (e.g. the threat of euro liabilities not remaining denominated in euros) on so Greek and other euro area members' debts and other financial instruments. As such, at least some of the stabilizing effects of Mario Draghi's famous "whatever it takes speech[5]" in July 2012 may have been put at risk this weekend.

This has significantly increased the political and financial onus on the euro area to agree to more and deeper institutional integration of the euro area in the short to medium term. Only further deepening of relations within the common currency area, including especially in fiscal affairs, can hope to restore the irreversibility of the common currency put at risk this weekend. The Five Presidents' Report[6] recommendations have taken a new urgency for the euro area now.

Recent events in the Greek sovereign debt crisis can therefore be expected to lead to an accelerated integration of the euro area, though not have material direct implications for EU institutions.

The Impact on European Institutions of the Upcoming UK Referendum on EU Membership

The upcoming UK referendum on EU membership is highly unlikely to lead to material and lasting changes to EU institutions for the reason that the referendum is overwhelmingly likely to be fought with the UK government, prime minister and main British opposition parties all actively campaigning to stay in the EU. As a result, the referendum is overwhelmingly likely to be a public "yes" to continued UK EU membership. There are three main explanations for this conclusion:

David Cameron and the UK Government Will Campaign For a Yes; it is a natural part of a rational negotiation strategy to extract maximum concessions for David Cameron to threaten his political opponents in the rest of the EU with potentially campaigning against UK membership in the referendum. He is, however, highly likely in the end to campaign for a yes in the referendum for several reasons:

1) Avoid severing ties between the Conservative Party and the vast majority of British businesses; while most UK businesses will, to avoid alienating any potential current or future customers, prefer to refrain from taking a public stance in the referendum, if forced to do so by a potential looming no vote, they will do so in favor of staying inside the European Union. Were David Cameron to actively campaign for a no in the referendum, this would lead to a very damaging split between the Conservative Party and its traditional financial support base

2) A no vote would be economically very damaging to the UK; one of the main reasons for bringing forward the UK referendum as much as possible is to remove the uncertainty surrounding the outcome and thus alleviate the confidence risks to future investments in the UK economy. At the same time, it is clear that a no vote in the referendum would usher in a period of acute uncertainty surrounding the UK economy and location for especially foreign direct investment (FDI) into the UK serving as a production facility for the entire EU economy. For a country with the largest current account deficit in the G-7 at about 5 percent of GDP (roughly double the level

[5] http://www.ecb.europa.eu/press/key/date/2012/html/sp120726.en.html
[6] http://ec.europa.eu/priorities/economic-monetary-union/docs/5-presidents-report_en.pdf

in the United States), a no vote would hence be a source of potential financial instability for the UK both in the short and long term. Judging from prior comments from large foreign investors in the UK, it seems clear that the UK would stand to lose not only a sizable part of its future inward FDI, but also see a number of its main current foreign investors leave in the case of a vote to leave the EU. This would, apart from the City of London, pose substantial challenges for a number of large UK cities, which today hosts sizable FDI facilities

A Favorable Economic Context; the UK economy is currently projected to grow at 2.4 in 2015 and 2.2 percent in 2016, the most likely year of the referendum[7]. Combined with low levels of projected unemployment, low inflation forecasts and what will still then be a generally accommodating monetary policy by the Bank of England, the UK referendum date is likely to be chosen by David Cameron amidst a broadly favorable economic situation in the United Kingdom. This will most likely avoid the risk that the UK population will vote against the recommendation of the UK government to punish it for poor economic circumstances around the time of the referendum.

EU Law Is Very Flexible When Political Will Is Present; probably the defining characteristic of European integration is the complexity of the EU's institutional design and decision making processes. However, this very complexity is merely a reflection of the intricate calibration of pooling of national sovereignty – quite uniquely in the world politically possible – among EU member states to precisely match the always conflicting forces of integration and national self-determination. As a result, the EU has over time developed a number of legal instruments to incorporate particular national sensitivities within the overarching EU legal Treaty architecture.

In principle, EU law is valid throughout the 28 member states. Yet, in a number of cases, individual member states have secured a so called "legal opt-out" from specific elements of the EU Treaty, excepting them from having to implement relevant policies at home. Currently, four EU members have such explicit legal opt-outs; Denmark (four), Ireland (two), Poland (one) and indeed already the United Kingdom with another four opt-outs. Currently the UK has official legal opt-outs in the Lisbon Treaty from of the euro, the Schengen Agreement, Justice and Home Affairs, and parts of the Charter of Fundamental Rights of the European Union.

Rather than secure a legal opt-out exempting a member state from a specific element of European law, EU law also has introduced the legal guarantee, or specification/clarification to assuage any fears in a given member state related to the interpretation of a given legal statute. This removes the opportunity for alternative subsequent interpretations to emerge in a specific area.

Lastly, reflecting the tremendously time consuming process and political difficulty of negotiating and ratifying a new EU Treaty, examples exists from Ireland of having specific opt-outs and legal guarantees added as a protocol to the existing EU Treaty (adding protocols does not require re-ratification in all member states of the entire Treaty), against the promise to introduce them into the actual Treaty only at the time of the next future broader Treaty change.

---

[7] The political guarantee issued by Prime Minister Cameron merely states that the referendum has to be held by 2017, but it could come earlier.

In short, the EU legal framework is a highly flexible animal, when EU leaders require some flexibility and legal finessing to overcome a particular political problem. Given how Germany and many other EU members have expressed their clear political interest in seeing the UK remain a member of the EU, there can be no doubt that the full arsenal of EU legal flexibility around the Treaty will be made available to David Cameron. Everything except revisions of the existing EU Treaty that would require re-ratification will be on the table.

There will consequently be ample opportunities for David Cameron to secure politically symbolic and important, as well as legally binding, changes to the EU laws governing the economy of the United Kingdom as part of the now ongoing negotiations. Outright Treaty changes would be impossible, as would the undermining or opt-out of core EU principles. Yet, there is little reason to believe that the rest of the EU would not offer the UK government Danish or Irish style opt-outs of specific issue areas of a sufficient political, economic and legal scope to secure David Cameron's agreement and support for a referendum campaign yes.

What such areas would be will be revealed as part of the negotiations, but could include the UK opting out of things like the EU Working Time Directive[8], EU rules for social benefits to the dependents of recent arrivals, securing a legal guarantee that the City of London will not be discriminated against as the euro area banking/capital markets union deepens, or perhaps even a symbolic UK opt-out of the "ever closer union" phrase at the beginning of the EU Treaty.

In the end, the upcoming UK referendum about membership of the EU is therefore not likely to materially affect the function or scope of existing EU institutions and will not set in motion a general renegotiation of the EU Treaty. Instead the referendum and the associated negotiations are likely to lead to the UK becoming exempt from some elements of existing EU law through legal opt-outs and/or legal clarifications and Treaty protocols.

The Impact on European Institutions of the Growing Electoral Success of Euro-skeptic Parties

In recent years, many EU countries have witnessed the growth of new parties, which when compared to the traditional mainstream center-right and center-left parties in Europe can be classified as broadly euro-skeptic in their political outlook. This includes parties like UKIP in the UK, True Finns in Finland, Five Star Movement in Italy, Freedom Party in Austria, Party for Freedom in the Netherlands, Danish People's Party in Denmark, Front Nationale in France, or AfD in Germany.

At the same time, however, it must be kept in mind that European parliamentary systems have historically often operated successfully with very large anti-establishment – and indeed to a degree anti-democratic – representation in national and the European parliament. Prior to 1989, this was seen with the often sizable communist parties in national legislatures and in the European parliament a host of nationalist anti-EU parties and movements. The height of mainstream party political dominance in

---

[8] Ironically, the UK was exempt from the Working Time Directive from the introduction of the Maastricht Treaty in 1993 until Tony Blair's government opted back in 1998.

Europe during the 1990s and early 2000s is therefore to a degree a historical anomaly, while the recent growth of euro-skeptic parties represents almost a return to the historical political norm.

With the exception of Hungary and in January 2015 Greece, the new wave of euro-skeptic parties in Europe has generally not seen their popularity break out of the historical range of up to an around 25 percent representation in parliament[9]. These levels are in parliamentary systems, where the mainstream centrist parties general agree on the broad lines of European policy, not an immediate threat to the stability and continuity of day-to-day European policy making. Simply put, in European parliamentary systems it is largely irrelevant what a 25-30 percent parliamentary minority might favor, when the remaining 70-75 percent of parliaments wish to generally maintain the status quo.

There is no immediate reason – outside extraordinary economic crisis situations like currently in Greece or latently irredentist polities like Hungary nourishing populism – to believe that euro-skeptic parties are going to continue to grow beyond their historical political range and into effective governing majorities across Europe. This is due to the narrowness of the core shared political message of many of these parties, which apart from shared opposition to EU integration and more recently austerity demands, represent a mixture of both right- and leftwing populism. Many – though not all and for instance not Syriza – of the new euro-skeptic parties combine rightwing anti-immigration platforms with traditionally leftwing pro-welfare state policies. This can be described as a welfare chauvinistic political platform, advocating a strong and activist role for the state in protecting the social welfare of only the native population. This policy mix has generally and successfully targeted the lower-skilled segments of European electorates, yet has to date failed to extend much beyond these groups. Slightly simplified, this group of euro-skeptic parties will often be the largest blue-collar parties in Europe today, but will fail to become majoritarian parties due to the relatively small share of these voters in the total electorates.

At the same time, even if euro-skeptic parties are unlikely to be able to regularly wield governing power in Europe, their recent rise has already had and will continue to have important shaping influences on EU institutions through several channels. First of all, their stronger political voices very significantly raise the political hurdles for further revisions of the EU Treaty, and in particular the prospects for unavoidable referenda successfully approving such treaty reforms. This means that the EU for the foreseeable future will have to continue to function within the broad legal framework laid down in the 2009 Lisbon Treaty. As witnessed since the Greek crisis began, this does not present the EU and especially the euro area with insurmountable political obstacles for new integrationist measures in emergencies, though clearly adds greatly to their complexity and potentially slows down their negotiation. Going forward, the EU's ability to act decisively in the face of new emerging challenges will therefore be gradually more constrained by what will become an ever more outdated legal foundation in the Lisbon Treaty.

Secondly, the rise of euro-skeptic parties pose a particular challenge for the euro area, as it is the common currency which (as described above) faces the most acute need for further both political and economic integration. The political hurdles to achieve for instance even just an embryonic fiscal union

---

[9] See also Nicolas Veron (2014) for data for this for the European Parliament at http://blogs.piie.com/realtime/?p=4372

complete with common political decision making over some budgetary issues, some potential meaningful euro area counter-cyclical fiscal policy tools and the prospects of issuance of joint debt securities (Eurobonds) will be very high. This is especially so for periods where the absence of acute economic crisis will cause European policymakers and electorates to hesitate in surrendering the required additional national sovereignty to such new necessary institutions. The euro area is therefore at risk from the rise of euro-skeptic parties of remaining an essentially unfinished and hence inherently more unstable institutional project even in the medium to long term. This will again in the future expose EU institutions to the same risk faced in recent years of Europe's entire political energy devoted to stabilizing the common currency, while neglecting the of other policy challenges facing the EU.

In sum, the recent (re)emergence of euro-skeptic parties across Europe will therefore not materially affect the overall direction of EU policies, but will greatly slowdown the adaptability of the EU's institutional design by making further EU Treaty revisions very difficult.

———————

Mr. ROHRABACHER. Thank all of you for your testimony today. I will start with a few questions, and then we will proceed to our other members as well.

So you are saying that the British are going to vote to stay in the EU.

You are more pessimistic about that, correct?

Mr. WALT. Actually, no, if I had to bet, I would bet that the U.K. Would remain in as well, but as was just said——

Mr. ROHRABACHER. Okay. So all three of you are thinking the U.K. Will stay in there, all right.

I was interested in this talk about EU being flexible. And I think one of the things that I believe is being criticized is that Brussels actually is trying to manage things from a central location, and that is creating a lot of resentment among people. Just as here in the United States, some people are a little bit concerned about the fact that Washington, DC, is coopting various political decisions that used to belong to the States.

But none of you are convinced that this in and of itself is a resentment about the centralization of power that will lead to the demise of the EU or at least some crisis for the EU. However, what about what you just touched on, the immigration, the effect of immigration into these countries? And, quite frankly, there is a lot of people in our country that don't believe that people who have come here illegally should be receiving government benefits and the benefits of our society, even jobs.

Is the immigration that is going on in the EU now changing the fundamental nature of those countries to the point that the EU— these were different countries then that joined the EU 30, 40 years ago. So is immigration going to change that? Maybe a little bit— 30 seconds for each one of you on that.

Mr. MCCORMICK. Yes, it is. I mean, there is a lot of similarities between the kind of problems we face here and the kind of problems that the Europeans are facing as well. The immigration issue is more complicated for them because there is a religious factor, and there is a racial factor involved. So part of the concern about immigration is motivated by religious and racial extremism. But the number of immigrants in Europe, as a percent of the population, is less than the number of immigrants in this country.

Mr. ROHRABACHER. Of course, we are a nation of immigrants, so, I mean, we represent every race, religion, and ethnic group. We are very proud of that. So it wouldn't have that much of an impact as opposed to a homogenous society.

Dr. Walt, what do you think?

Mr. WALT. One is, Europe historically has done a poorer job of assimilating immigrants than the United States has. That has been one of our great successes throughout our history. And, second, this has to be understood in the context of a continent really that has experienced very slow economic growth ever since the financial crisis.

So in addition to having significant problems of immigration, some degree of violence stemming from that, you have the concerns of unemployment, the concerns that immigrants from Eastern Europe are taking jobs away. Whether that is correct or not, the perception, I think, is widespread in parts of Europe. And that in turn reinforces the popularity of some of these right-wing nationalists or Eurosceptic parties.

So, in a sense, the inability to deal with the immigration problem may make the Euroskeptisim problem worse as well.

Mr. KIRKEGAARD. I would say that I think the main political impact of immigration in the EU right now is actually both the scale but also to relative novelty of this because the scale is actually very large. If you look at the number of permanent legal immigrants coming into the EU since in the 21st century, it is actually about twice the level of green card holders coming into the United States.

But, secondly, this is happening to countries that historically does not have the tradition that the United States has. These are countries that were traditionally very homogenous, have sort of light culture, nationally dominant cultures, and therefore, as was mentioned, these countries have historically done poorer in terms of integrating these immigrant communities.

So if, indeed, the EU policy is a more, let's say, liberal policy of accepting this immigration into these countries, that would work to undercut—the nationalists within those countries would then be a more opposed to the EU. Is that correct? You understand? In other words, if the EU is pushing for a higher level of acceptance of immigration, and the people of those countries, because they are more homogenous, do not want them, that would actually be weakening the EU. Is that correct?

Mr. KIRKEGAARD. I think it would depend very much on where you are in the EU. If you are in Italy right now, where the number of illegal immigrants crossing the Mediterranean is very, very large, you would actually campaign and be very much in favor of the EU taking charge of this migration and trying to spread it out throughout the entire Union, thereby loosening the burden of Italy specifically.

Whereas, of course, if you are in Finland, you would probably have the opposite opinion about sort of sending this up to be a policy area dictated or governed by EU.

Mr. ROHRABACHER. Okay.

Very quickly, the agreement with the Greek Government is thumbs up or thumbs down for the EU? Is it positive or negative long term?

Mr. MCCORMICK. Thumbs up.

Mr. ROHRABACHER. Dr. Walt.

Mr. WALT. I think it is largely irrelevant. I think it is a short-term Band-Aid, but I don't see in this agreement yet the solution to Greek's ultimate economic problems.

Mr. ROHRABACHER. But is it going to be a thumbs down then?

Mr. WALT. Then I believe we will see a replay of what we have just witnessed at some point in the future and how many times Europe can go through this series of brinkmanship before you finally do get a Greek exit remains to be seen. But I wouldn't be confident that patience is infinite.

Mr. KIRKEGAARD. Thumbs up. I think the political significance of a country that, having lost a third or perhaps up to a third of its GDP, now still would, I believe, in the coming days will find a significant political majority to implement this deal—and therefore stay in the euro area—I don't think should be easily dismissed.

Mr. ROHRABACHER. All right.

Mr. Meeks, you may proceed.

Mr. MEEKS. Thank you.

Let me make sure that—and I think I got it right. But I think that, Dr. McCormick, is it important for the EU to stay together?

Mr. MCCORMICK. Yes.

Mr. MEEKS. Dr. Walt.

Mr. WALT. It would be better for us if it did and better for Europe if it did.

Mr. MEEKS. So it is better for us and Europe?

Mr. WALT. Yes.

Mr. MEEKS. So it is better for everyone?

Mr. KIRKEGAARD. Absolutely better for everyone.

Mr. MEEKS. So, now let's just talk about dealing with this Greek problem for a second because some say to deal with the problem, if you listen to the Greek Prime Minister, he came in on a mandate of no austerity. And yet, in this agreement, there is austerity. Do you see any debt relief in this agreement? Because some will say—and I will go to—I guess, you are the economist here—that if Greece is ever going to get back on its feet, it is not just austerity. It is austerity with debt relief so that it can begin to grow again. Can you talk a little bit about that?

Mr. KIRKEGAARD. Yeah. I mean, there is no doubt that you need a combination of the two. You need some degree of fiscal rectitude because Greece is a country that historically has run very large and persistent government deficits. But given where the debt is now, you clearly also need debt relief.

And I actually do believe that there is very credible prospects for debt relief included in this agreement because what it does is that it basically tells the Greeks that if you agree to a new bailout program, following the first successful review of that program, we can have a discussion of debt relief, meaning that the debt relief comes only as a reward, so to speak, for good behavior.

And then the other issue is that we need to be clear about what debt relief entails. I don't believe you will see an actual haircut on the debt, but I certainly do believe that you will see the Greek Government debt being restructured in a way so that they may not have to pay any interest or amortization for 30 years. The maturity of the debt may well be extended to 60 years or beyond that. So the actual cost of the debt—which incidentally is already below the levels of interest paid by the U.S. Federal Government, despite much higher gross debt levels—becomes more or less a non-issue, in my opinion, for the ability of the Greek economy to grow.

And then, finally, I should note that—and this is where the U.S. influence will be very important—part of the reason that the European Union will be compelled—or sorry the euro area will be compelled to do this probably by the first quarter of next year is that they are seeking IMF cofinancing, about one-third financing for this program starting March next year. That can only happen, in my opinion, that should only happen if they by that time have done a restructuring of the Greek debt.

Mr. MEEKS. Anybody want to add anything or take away anything from that?

Mr. WALT. I will just say, I am not as optimistic for several reasons. First of all, Greece's debt is now in excess of $300 billion or so. This new relief package is about $80 billion, I believe, somewhere along there. But most of that money is simply going to get recycled back to European financial institutions of one kind or another. It is not a stimulus program for Greece; it just allows them to keep servicing their loan. So it does nothing by itself to actually get the Greek economy to be more productive at all.

There is no debt relief in this package yet. It is promised out there. And what the Europeans are now asking Greece to do is suffer a little bit more, in fact, suffer a lot more with the prospect that then things will improve at some point down the road.

What I am, I guess, still baffled by is if the Greek reform was so easy, why hasn't it happened already? It has been, you know, 5 or 6 years where they have had multiple opportunities. It is clearly politically extremely difficult for the Greeks to do this. And to expect them to do it having inflicted even more pain on them, I think we are as likely to see essentially sharper political divisions within Greece, as opposed to suddenly all linking arms and beginning a serious reform program.

So, again, I hope this package works, but I am not confident that it will.

Mr. MCCORMICK. One line of thought that is not often explored and discussed in the Greek debt crisis is the responsibility that Greece itself holds for getting itself into this current mess. Greece should never have been allowed into the U.N. in the first place. That was a mistake because it didn't meet the terms of membership.

It had mismanaged its economy before it was allowed into the euro. Being allowed into the euro just made matters worse because it was allowed to borrow money at a lower interest rate than there have been before. It then went off on a debt-laden spending spree which made all of its bad previous habits even worse.

So my optimism about Greece is based on the fact that I think the Greek people and the Greek Government are going to get to the point where they realize they have to clean house; they have to manage their economy effectively, as effectively as some of their other European neighbors have. And whatever the terms of the bailout or the debt relief or the terms of some of these deals that are done, I think what we are seeing here is a very hard learning experience for the Greek people about how to manage a modern economy.

And I am a bit nervous about saying this because I am not sure it is a very popular idea, but I think the European Union and the eurozone—and the Germans—attract more criticism than I think they deserve. And I think we have to look at what the Greeks have done to bring this upon themselves.

Mr. MEEKS. I am out of time.

Mr. ROHRABACHER. All right.

Colonel Cook.

Mr. COOK. Thank you, Mr. Chairman.

I talked in my opening statement that I was going to ask you about the Russian situation and the fact that, not just in terms of the EU but NATO having that economic olive branch out there: Hey, we got the money. We can help you out.

Can you comment on that possibility of—somebody mentioned—I think the doctor talked about that in Hungary—and you can include that in other countries, that—because their economic situation might be interested in that handout.

Mr. WALT. I think, given the conflict we have with Russia now over Ukraine, Russia has quite cleverly and understandably used its various assets, including offers of money to try and diminish European unity and to some degree NATO unity to prevent extensions of economic sanctions to try and weaken Western resolve. And as I indicated in my initial statement, one of the problems here is that there isn't really a consensus in Europe today on just how serious the Russian threat really is.

I think everyone acknowledges that it is a problem. There is no real support for Russia's behavior in Ukraine. But whether it is a new cold war or whether it is the return of the battle of Soviet Union, there is certainly no agreement there. And I think most Europeans actually don't see it as nearly as serious a problem. Perhaps the Baltic states do but hardly anybody else in Europe.

So I think you will see Russia attempt to dangle various blandishments in front of some European countries, including Greece, and that is a way they can exploit it. I don't think it is going to, you know, cause the EU to dissolve tomorrow, but it is an additional source of centrifugal force within the union as a whole.

Mr. KIRKEGAARD. I guess I would be slightly less optimistic or pessimistic, depending on—but I don't basically think that Russia has much to offer Greece in the real world. The reality is that Greece needs so much money, that Vladimir Putin doesn't have that.

Just to give you an example, if there had been no agreement over this weekend, the European Central Bank would have pulled out 89 billion euros from the Greek banking system, and it would probably, in fact, need considerably more than that to keep these banks afloat. And Vladimir Putin, in my opinion, doesn't have that much money in liquid reserves. And even if he did, I am highly skeptical that he would be willing to put that much cash into Greece.

So Vladimir Putin, therefore, in terms of, shall we say, offering a material difference to the acute economic crisis that Greeks face right now, really doesn't have much to offer. And I think you can see that, in fact, that at the end of the day when the negotiations in the European Union about extending the current sanctions on Russia was up for debate where unanimity is required, the Greek Government basically posed no particular objection.

Mr. COOK. Thank you.

Dr. McCormick.

Mr. McCORMICK. You know, in my opening statement, I said one of the great benefits or achievements of the European Union was the expansion of free markets and democracy, both within Europe and outside Europe. Greece is one of those cases where it joined the European Union after having spent some time under military government with its democratic credentials in question.

I think the benefits that Greece has seen over the last 30, 40 years, have been part of the European economic community, European Union. It would be very difficult to imagine anything that Russia or specifically Putin could offer that would be better than what Greece has now, even in spite of the fact the Greeks are going through terrible times at the moment. The political and economic benefits that have been part of this enormous partnership are so much greater than having any kind of association with something like Putin's Russia.

Mr. COOK. Thank you.

I am going to a conference, a NATO conference this week, and we will see whether they have the same optimism.

I want to talk about the borders and terrorism. And if X amount of terrorists get in one country, particularly one that is easier to get into, that they all share that the same logo of being able to enter another country, is the EU going to strengthen that, or are they going to continue that policy as a whole, particularly in light of increased terrorism? And I am looking at ISIS and some of the other elements.

Mr. WALT. As I mentioned, one of the concerns I have is the degree to which external events, events around the European continent are beginning to impinge upon Europe in new ways, and you have just referred to them.

The so-called Schengen principles, which allow internal migration without real restriction, without border controls in much of the European Union, is a major achievement and has been an economic benefit but, I also think, has contributed to a general sense of being a European community. And there have been calls in recent months for tightening those various restrictions, to reimposing some of these border controls to deal precisely with this problem.

I personally think that would be a mistake because I don't believe the problem that Europe faces or the threat Europe faces from various forms of extremism is so great as to warrant that decision. But politics is not always rational, and I can easily see that if there were one or two more incidents in Europe, even if they were of a rather small scale, you might see more momentum up to start reimposing some of the border controls. And that would be a step back from one of the achievements that the community had made in recent years.

Mr. COOK. Thank you.

I yield back.

Mr. ROHRABACHER. Mr. Sires.

Mr. SIRES. Thank you, Mr. Chairman.

You know, the more I read and the more I try to learn about Greece, it is just mind boggling. And then you have all these rumors out there that I don't know what is true or what is not true, about the percentage of tax collection that they have, about supposedly it is cheaper to take a cab across Greece than to take a train because the trains, the way they are run, the transit system, I mean, it is just—and then you talk to other people, and they tell you that the underground economy in Greece is thriving.

Now, is that accurate, the underground economy?

Mr. KIRKEGAARD. Yes, that would generally be, in my opinion, correct. It is both very large and has historically been very large, and it has certainly grown a lot bigger in the last 5 years.

Mr. SIRES. And this is just a reason to avoid paying taxes?

Mr. KIRKEGAARD. Yeah, this is to avoid paying taxes but also to avoid being subject to a whole other host, a range of social and labor market regulations.

Mr. SIRES. Would you agree with that?

Mr. MCCORMICK. The most recent figure I saw for 2009, the OECD said that approximately 25 percent of the GDP of Greece was based on the gray market. By nature, the gray market and the black market are very difficult to measure, but the OECD, 25 percent.

Mr. SIRES. So but this is something that has been going on in Greece for a very long time. So this is like the old expression, you know: You have an old dog; how can you teach him new tricks? You know, how are you going to do that?

Mr. MCCORMICK. In brief, I think the costs of reorganizing their economy in a sensible, modern fashion—sorry—the benefits are much greater than the costs of continuing to do what they are doing now. They can see the costs now. The terrible things that the Greeks are having to go through, the costs they are having to pay for years of this kind of activity are abundantly clear to most Greek people.

Mr. SIRES. Do you agree with that?

Mr. KIRKEGAARD. Yes, I would absolutely agree with that. And I think the way to look at Greece is actually not through the lenses of thinking of it as just in an economic crisis. I think a closer comparison is actually sort of 1989, the collapse of communism because what has happened in Greece in the last number of years is essentially that the existing economic and political system, I would argue, that was put in place after the end of the military regime in the 1970s has, for all respective purposes, collapsed.

So what you need is actually an extensive amount of fundamental capacity building and nation building in order for this country to reemerge, quite frankly, as a modern, functioning market economy.

Mr. WALT. I would just add that when I hear the word ''nation building,'' it always makes me nervous because I think we now know that that is a very difficult, time-consuming, and unpredictable enterprise. And if you consider the scale of reform that has to take place in Greece for this to work—we have to have a complete reform of their tax system; complete deregulation of many of their industries, revision of the pension system; and this all has to happen in a period where there is no slack, right, where the economy has essentially been in free fall for quite some time now—you need both political will to pull that off; you need lots of competent people to pull that off. And we are expecting Greece to do that in very rapid order, right.

This is a very large demand that essentially the rest of the European Union is making. It may be necessary. It may be the right prescription, but you can't be confident that they will pull it off, even if they try hard.

Mr. SIRES. You know, as I listen to you, to me, why would I throw money in there? Why would I even insist in trying to——

Mr. WALT. Well, I think as——

Mr. SIRES. I know what you said, that it is important and all that, but they don't seem capable of doing it. I mean, Portugal and

Ireland, they got some money, and they seem to be getting their act straightened out pretty much. But I don't see anything going on in Greece where that gives me the confidence, if I were a European country, to go in there and say: Well, you know, let's throw in another $95 billion in the hope that in the next 50 years, that it will get better.

Mr. McCORMICK. It does seem like throwing good money after bad. But I guess my question would be: What is the alternative?

Mr. SIRES. Let them go on their own.

I mean, why——

Mr. McCORMICK. Then you are going to have more disruption right on the border of the European Union. You are going to have another unstable country causing difficulties for everybody right on the border. Surely, it is best to invest and work with the Greek Government because, remember, you know, the Greek Government is meeting with its 27 peers all the time at meetings. They are talking about common issues. So to be brought into this family of negotiation, this new style of negotiation, surely better to bring them into the room and talk to them than to throw them out and say, Good luck.

Mr. KIRKEGAARD. There is a significant degree of political self-preservation in this as well because if you do not give Greece a new third bailout, then the Greek Government will default on all the existing loans that the eurozone has made to them, which is 240 billion euros or something like that, which means that the Germans and others would have to admit to their own voters that this was actually not a loan that at some point in the future might be repaid but a gift.

Mr. SIRES. I mean, Greece existed before the eurozone, right?

Mr. KIRKEGAARD. Correct.

Mr. WALT. And as I think one thing we would all agree on this panel is it was a mistake to let Greece into the eurozone in the first place. It may even have been a mistake to create the euro given it lacked the political institutions to actually make a common currency work.

The disagreement you are hearing a little bit on the panel is, of course, replicated inside Europe itself, from those who think it would actually be bettor for rest of the EU to allow Greece to Grexit, to leave the common currency, despite all of the consequences that have just been referred to and those who think that those consequences could be so severe that it has to be avoided. That has essentially been the disagreement between France and Germany over the past few months.

Mr. SIRES. Thank you very much.

Thank you, Mr. Chairman, for the courtesy.

Mr. ROHRABACHER. Sort of like those people who think it might have been a good idea to let Puerto Rico be independent.

Mr. Brooks.

Mr. BROOKS. Thank you, Mr. Chairman.

I have been pondering American history with Europe while we have been listening to your testimony and Q&A back and forth. It seems, after World War II, for 47 years when there was not a European community, our relationship with Europe was good. Then we had the EU created, 7 years' worth of phase-in, and the euro currency comes into play, roughly 1999, and now we have had 16 years thereafter, and our relationship has been good. So it seems to me, either way, America's relationship with Europe has done well with and without the euro.

So, to me, the European Union issue is more of a focal point for the European nations, and they should be the deciders of their fate. And I am curious about a comment that was made that the "European Union is better for the USA."

And my question is, why? What can you share with us that would help convince me that it is in America's best interest to have a European Union as opposed to not having one in as much as our relationship with Europe was good in both contexts?

Mr. WALT. I think I said that so I will take a swing at it. First of all, the EU, whatever its current problems may be, is a major economic block in the world and a major trading partner for the United States.

Mr. BROOKS. Was that good for us or bad for us if they collectively have more strength as they negotiate trade agreements with the United States?

Mr. WALT. But a prosperous European economy and a European economy that is growing is one that American businesses can send and sell more products to and American investors can send their money and make money investing in Europe.

Mr. BROOKS. Do you have any data that shows that Europe was growing slower before the EU as opposed to after the EU?

Mr. WALT. It has grown at different—in the 1990s, it actually grew quite well, as did we. It has had problems since 2008 as we have. We have recovered more quickly than Europe has.

Mr. BROOKS. I know this is little bit outside the framework of this hearing, but do you have any data that backs that up——

Mr. WALT. I don't have——

Mr. BROOKS. The history of that—well, we are talking since 1945, so that would be somewhere in the neighborhood of 70 years.

Mr. WALT. The lowering of trade barriers throughout Europe, which was part of the original European project, clearly helped stimulate economic recovery throughout the 1950s, 1960s, so it was very beneficial for Europe to essentially allow free trade within Europe and allow their economies to grow.

Second thing is that, as has been said here, the European Union has been a source of stability within Europe, and the community was also very instrumental in helping the transition from communism, and that is good for the United States because it has been, until relatively recently, a part of the world where we didn't have to worry as much post the breakup of the Soviet Union.

There are other parts of the world that we have been much more concerned with, and if Europe began to spiral back toward real national rivalries, American policymakers would have to spend more time worrying about that and less worrying about other problems.

And then, third, I would say that, you know, Europe has been a strategic partner of ours for a long time. And if Europe is internally preoccupied and economically weaker and increasingly divided, then when we try to deal with other strategic problems in the world, we are going to find we are going to get even less help from Europe than we do now.

Mr. BROOKS. One of the important aspects of our relationship with Europe is our military alliance, particularly NATO, and it seems that under the European Union, defense spending by the collective of European nations has declined, as opposed to when they weren't a part of the European Union, thus making them less able to help America in troubled spots around the globe. I just mention that as a concern of mine.

I want to focus more in my remaining time on the Greek bailout impact on America. We have had now our third bailout. Our first one was in 2010, second one was in 2012, and now we are 2015, and there is some hope that maybe this one will stick when the two prior ones did not.

What is the monetary exposure to the United States of these bailouts failing?

Mr. KIRKEGAARD. I guess I can take a stab at that. The direct exposure to the United States to the Greek bailouts comes through the IMF and the approximately 17 percent ownership or shareholding that the U.S. Has.

Mr. BROOKS. 17.69 percent.

Mr. KIRKEGAARD. And that—given currently that exposure is about 25—I believe $25 billion, so 17 percent of 16 to 17 percent of that.

However, as was seen in the last—in the agreement this weekend, actually, the Europeans made it very explicit that they are going to pay—essentially give Greece the money so that they can repay the IMF, which means that, in my opinion——

Mr. BROOKS. Very quickly, in my remaining few seconds, is the IMF involved in the third bailout?

Mr. KIRKEGAARD. I believe they will be, yes.

Mr. BROOKS. That you will increase our exposure to the extent the IMF is supplying funds for the third bailout?

Mr. KIRKEGAARD. It will not necessarily increase it because existing loans will be repaid simultaneously so there——

Mr. BROOKS. Do you know the net?

Mr. KIRKEGAARD. Sorry?

Mr. BROOKS. Do you know the net, is it going to go up or down because we have got the old bailout numbers and now we have got the new bailout numbers and payoffs of some of the old, but we have got all the new, is it going to be a net up or down?

Mr. KIRKEGAARD. I don't know what the requests from the Europeans will be. It also depends on the size of Greek privatization proceeds, et cetera. But I would say that for the next 3 to 4 years, probably it will be about even, after which it will begin to decline quite rapidly.

Mr. BROOKS. Mr. Chairman, my time is expired. Thank you for the indulgence and the extra 45 seconds.

Mr. ROHRABACHER. So we have the—so the United States will be paying for the some of the bailout because we are part of the International Monetary Fund. No? What is it?

Mr. BROOKS. Yeah, we are; 17.69 percent is our quota ownership of the International Monetary Fund. So whatever the assets are in the IMF and their obligations to Greece, since we are one of the owners, there is an impact on the United States.

Mr. ROHRABACHER. So of this—so what is your guess, then, of the—if you say that there is going to be a certain amount of bail-out, and how much of that is the United States going to end up paying?

Mr. KIRKEGAARD. Well, the range that was mentioned in this——

Mr. ROHRABACHER. Through this, you know——

Mr. KIRKEGAARD. The range that was mentioned of the agreement over the weekend was 60—or 82 to 86 billion euros, which is about 90—a couple of—just over $90 billion.

Mr. ROHRABACHER. Right. And so——

Mr. KIRKEGAARD. And then the—however, subtracted from that will be whatever the proceeds—a certain number of Greek Government privatization proceeds from privatizing state-owned enterprises, et cetera. Now, how much that will be is unknown, but the target is 50. I certainly don't believe they would reach 50, but let's say it is 20. That takes you down to sort of in the mid 70s or $70 billion. So one-third of that would be for the IMF to cover.

Mr. ROHRABACHER. And how much of that of us? So one-third of that is—what—20 billion, $25 billion?

Mr. KIRKEGAARD. Yeah, give and take. It will be—let's say it is 22, and then 16 percent of the 22.

Mr. ROHRABACHER. 16 percent of it. Now, what does that leave? That leaves us about $5 billion just about?

Mr. KIRKEGAARD. Yeah, something like that.

Mr. ROHRABACHER. Okay.

Mr. KIRKEGAARD. Give or take.

Mr. ROHRABACHER. So isn't that wonderful, we are getting to bail out Greece and our friends over in Europe for $5 billion? Isn't that wonderful? We can't find any way to use that money anyway, just, you know——

Mr. WALT. It is important to recognize that if the bailout deal were to work, then it is not a handout. It is a loan that gets repaid. All right, so the question really is, do you think that this is likely to turn Greece around, finally allow it to begin to pay off its debts, lead to a restructuring of the debt, and we all live happily ever after?

Mr. ROHRABACHER. When you talk about this debt—excuse me, and I am going to go to our last member of the panel here, but what is—these banks. We are talking about we are bailing out these—the European banks. These people are being bailed out, said the banks are actually getting the money. Are these privately held banks or are these banks that are owned by the Government of France and England, and et cetera?

Mr. KIRKEGAARD. Well, in this instance, the current bailout that is under discussion is actually not private banks that own the debt. There was that issue back in 2010, where there were clearly some European banks that benefitted from that. They were mostly private banks in France and elsewhere.

But, clearly, the European government entered into this process because they were afraid that otherwise they would have to bail out these banks themselves and therefore make them, so to speak, publically available.

Mr. ROHRABACHER. So we are not bailing out any private—this money for bailing out Greece does not include money that is going to privately owned banks.

Mr. KIRKEGAARD. No. I mean, there are——

Mr. ROHRABACHER. Is that right? The other gentleman, is that true? Is that true?

Mr. WALT. I don't think that is entirely true. It depends sort of what you mean by privately held banks. Some of this money will help Greek banks that have no cash on hand at present. It is why they——

Mr. ROHRABACHER. It sort of have—makes it even worse, doesn't it, as far as we are.

Ms. Gabbard.

Ms. GABBARD. Thank you. Thank you, Mr. Chairman.

Dr. Walt, just wanted to follow up on some of your previous comments about being better for us in the U.S. If EU stays together—EU stays together. If you could—if you could answer the question in the opposite way of talking about how we can measure what the impact on our economy would be if the EU completely dissolves or if it ends up that the U.K. Ends up exiting the EU, what kind of impact would that have for us?

Mr. WALT. In terms of purely in economic terms, I think that that would be a blow to the eurozone and the EU in general as an economic actor. I think it would lead to slower economic growth within Europe, which is already relatively low, but that, in turn, reduces economic opportunities for the United States because if the euro—the EU is growing at ½ percent a year, then there are far fewer American firms for consulting. There are far fewer Europeans who are going to be buying American products.

So we would be better off if Europe had a rapidly vigorously growing economy and a healthy demand for American products.

Ms. GABBARD. Do we have any idea, with a little more specificity, on what kind of impact that would be? Obviously, you are saying there would be some loss here, but I am just trying to look for a little bit more specifics.

Mr. WALT. Yeah, I can't give you a figure, sort of macroeconomic estimate. I just don't have that, of what the actual impact on the U.S. economy would be. But I know that anything that hurts the European economy will also hurt the United States, not perhaps as much, but it has a negative effect on our economic prospects as well.

Ms. GABBARD. Okay.

Mr. MCCORMICK. It is very difficult to put numbers on this, but I mean, the United States now is dealing with one economic block, so when the U.S. trades with the European Union, negotiates with the European Union, trade negotiator, it is 1-on-1. The European Union breaks up, it is 1-on-28. There are 28 separate sets of bilateral agreements the U.S. has to work out with these countries.

Also, access to one big single market of 506 million people, a U.S. corporation doing business in any one of those 28 countries has access to the entire market. If this breaks down or splinters in some fashion, it adds that much more level of complication in terms of dealing with these entities.

Ms. GABBARD. With regard to what Prime Minister Cameron has before him, what do you assess he will be trying to renegotiate with regard to Britain's commitment to the EU?

Mr. KIRKEGAARD. I mean, I can take it. I mean, what he has—I mean, it is a little unclear precisely what he is asking for at this moment from the EU authority, but what he has mentioned is he would like to have Britain exempt from something called the working time directive, which is essentially a European regulation that says that you cannot work more than 48 hours a week.

Excuse me. And then there are other specific types of EU regulation or EU law that he would like the U.K. To be exempt from. He may also, it is alleged, seek to have the EU exempt from the sort of opening clause of the EU treaty, which talks about an ever closer union, which of course, would be purely symbolic politics. But, nonetheless, that of course is very important in a referendum campaign.

Ms. GABBARD. Thank you.

Thank you, Mr. Chairman.

Mr. ROHRABACHER. All right. We have a vote. So we are going to have to go very quickly here. Again, I just want to confirm this. So we are talking about, in this bailout, the Greek bailout, that about $5 billion will be—Americans can be—about $5 billion coming from our pockets.

I would like to again go back to who this money is going to. It is going—the bailout—first of all, is it accurate to say that the bankruptcy can be traced back to policies of the Greek Government?

Mr. KIRKEGAARD. In my opinion, yes.

Mr. WALT. Yes.

Mr. ROHRABACHER. Okay. So the Greek Government had policies that put us in a spot where banks—now, the banks that will be repaid now because they have been spending this money to keep the Greeks afloat. These banks are—you are saying they are not private banks; they are German banks, French banks and——

Mr. KIRKEGAARD. No, no. This is in 2010. Today, the people that are going to be repaid are, in fact, among other things, the IMF itself. It is also other official sector, the European Union—sorry, the euro area, and then a relatively small amount of total outstanding debt, about 20 percent of Greek debt is still held by private investors.

Mr. ROHRABACHER. Okay.

Mr. KIRKEGAARD. There is no direct, so to speak——

Mr. ROHRABACHER. So the last bailout, we saw private banks being—basically being given money bailed out, or excuse me. The bailout with the Greeks, but they give it to the private banks. Those private banks, are they profit-making institutions, or are they government-related institutions?

Mr. KIRKEGAARD. They will be mainly profit-making institutions.

Mr. ROHRABACHER. So how much was the last bailout?

Mr. KIRKEGAARD. The—well, the original bail—I mean, the total bailout so far is about 240 billion.

Mr. ROHRABACHER. $240 billion. Of that $240 billion, how much went do these private banks?

Mr. KIRKEGAARD. I think that that—I don't have a number off the top of my head, but I would say, if you look at the direct exposure that these banks had to the Greek debt that was restructured, which should also be known that these banks actually took, as all private debt holders did, a 50 percent haircut on this debt in 2012.

Mr. ROHRABACHER. Depends on if their haircut meant that they are still making a profit or whether it means they are going to eat into the resources. If a bank or if any other private institution, at least in our society, it is supposed to be, that if you take a risk, that is what you are—you are making your money because you are taking a risk in giving your money out. And if the Federal Government or if the European Union just simply bails out anybody who is taking a risk and makes up for it with public funds, I don't see why we are—why are they they making a profit then on this stuff? You are saying those banks didn't make a profit those years?

Mr. KIRKEGAARD. Well, I mean, I am saying that they are profit-making private enterprises. Whether—I would say that they definitely did not make a profit on the Greek debt holdings because they were compelled to take a sizeable debt restructuring, a 50-percent haircut back in 2012.

Mr. ROHRABACHER. Well, I am wondering—I could see why a lot of people would be very skeptical, regular working people, people who own small businesses or whatever, would be very skeptical in hearing about the transfer of all these billions of dollars and a lot of it going and bailing out really very, very wealthy people who control the banking system.

Mr. Meeks, you got one last——

Mr. MEEKS. Well, just, you know—sorry. It seems as though, from what I am hearing, that the risk to the United States, as far as us, it is minimal, if anything. It is not substantial. And the likelihood of us having to pay anything, especially with the special fund that the Europeans have set up to make sure the IMF is paid because the only exposure we would have is through the IMF, and that seems to be backed up already by the EU in this agreement saying that they are going to make sure that the IMF is paid. So, therefore, that basically would leave $0 that the United States is, you know, as far as being—is that not correct?

Mr. KIRKEGAARD. Yes, I absolutely—it is very important for me to emphasize that the IMF is the super senior creditor, and I believe that there will always be a very firm political commitment by the euro area to ensure that the IMF is paid back, and therefore, the actual exposure to the U.S. is, as you said, close to zero, effectively zero.

Mr. ROHRABACHER. I remember when we bailed out Mexico, but all the money——

Mr. MEEKS. You had your time already.

Mr. ROHRABACHER. But all the money went to American banks that never actually left our shores at all.

Mr. MEEKS. All I know is that what we had is a financial crisis in the United States also in 2008, and what we had to do was bail out our banks to keep our economy afloat. The banks ultimately paid things back, so this is not something that is unusual as far as, you know, dealing with the current economy. It is something, you know, they are not doing any differently than what we had to do.

We rebounded, and now we have got to get the reforms that are necessary and is best for the cost. You know, when you look at the EU as a whole for us, we are looking at what is in America's best interest, we got to hope that, you know, we are also doing what is in the Europeans' best interest, but I don't think—I don't know if you—but if you are looking just for what is America's best interest, it is for us to deal with Europe as a whole.

For example, one of the next big issues that we have to deal with in Congress is going to be another trade agreement called TTIP, and it would be best for the United States if we were negotiating that deal, that we are doing it with the EU as a whole because that then gives a greater market for our businesses to try to make sure that we are getting the best deal to create jobs here, et cetera. Is that not correct?

Mr. WALT. That is correct.

Mr. KIRKEGAARD. Correct.

Mr. MEEKS. Thank you.

Mr. ROHRABACHER. We have skeptics over here. I am one of them. All right. Thank you all very much.

Mr. Meeks, thank you. Thank you to our witnesses. We have a vote on, so we are going to have to run. God bless you. Thank you.

[Whereupon, at 3:20 p.m., the subcommittee was adjourned.]

APPENDIX

MATERIAL SUBMITTED FOR THE RECORD

SUBCOMMITTEE HEARING NOTICE
COMMITTEE ON FOREIGN AFFAIRS
U.S. HOUSE OF REPRESENTATIVES
WASHINGTON, D.C. 20515-6128

Subcommittee on Europe, Eurasia, and Emerging Threats
Dana Rohrabacher (R-CA), Chairman

July 7, 2015

TO: MEMBERS OF THE COMMITTEE ON FOREIGN AFFAIRS

You are respectfully requested to attend an OPEN hearing of the Committee on Foreign Affairs, to be held by the Subcommittee on Europe, Eurasia, and Emerging Threats in Room 2200 of the Rayburn House Office Building (and available on the Committee website at www.foreignaffairs.gov):

DATE: Tuesday, June 14, 2015

TIME: 2:00 p.m.

SUBJECT: The European Union's Future

WITNESSES: John McCormick, Ph.D.
                   Jean-Monnet Professor of European Union Politics
                   Indiana University-Purdue University Indianapolis

                   Stephen Walt, Ph.D.
                   Robert and Renee Belfer Professor of International Affairs
                   Belfer Center for Science and International Affairs
                   John F. Kennedy School of Government
                   Harvard University

                   Jacob Funk Kirkegaard, Ph.D.
                   Senior Fellow
                   Peterson Institute for International Economics

By Direction of the Chairman

The Committee on Foreign Affairs seeks to make its facilities accessible to persons with disabilities. If you are in need of special accommodations, please call 202/225-5021 at least four business days in advance of the event, whenever practicable. Questions with regard to special accommodations in general (including availability of Committee materials in alternative formats and assistive listening devices) may be directed to the Committee.

COMMITTEE ON FOREIGN AFFAIRS

MINUTES OF SUBCOMMITTEE ON _____ *EE&ET* _____ HEARING

Day___ *Tuesday* ___Date___ *July 14, 2015* ___Room_____ *2200* _____

Starting Time ___ *2:01 p.m.* ___ Ending Time ___ *3:20 p.m.* ___

Recesses |____| (____to ____) (____to ____) (____to ____) (____to ____) (____to ____) (____to ____)

Presiding Member(s)

Rep. Rohrabacher

Check all of the following that apply:

Open Session ☑   Electronically Recorded (taped) ☑
Executive (closed) Session ☐   Stenographic Record ☑
Televised ☑

TITLE OF HEARING:

The European Union's Future

SUBCOMMITTEE MEMBERS PRESENT:

Rep. Brooks, Rep, Cook, Rep, Meeks, Rep Sires.

NON-SUBCOMMITTEE MEMBERS PRESENT: *(Mark with an * if they are not members of full committee.)*

HEARING WITNESSES: Same as meeting notice attached? Yes ☑ No ☐
(If "no", please list below and include title, agency, department, or organization.)

STATEMENTS FOR THE RECORD: *(List any statements submitted for the record.)*

TIME SCHEDULED TO RECONVENE _____
or
TIME ADJOURNED ___ *3:20 p.m.* ___

Subcommittee Staff Director